The Tree of Life
for Kids

God's Promise of Salvation

Illustrated by
Janos Jantner

CONCORDIA PUBLISHING HOUSE · SAINT LOUIS

In the beginning, God made our world.
He made the sky, the sea, and dry land.
He put the sun, moon, and stars in the sky.
He filled the waters with fish and the sky with birds.
He made all the animals that live on land.
Then He made Adam and Eve.

God put Adam and Eve in the Garden of Eden.
He told them not to eat from one special tree;
    if they did, they would die.
When the serpent, Satan, said they would not die, they ate.
They were scared when God came to them,
    but God promised a child, Jesus, who would save us all.

God gave a baby to Abraham and Sarah, who were very old.

God promised that Isaac would be a very special boy.

When Isaac was a young man, God told Abraham to offer Isaac back to
   Him.

When Abraham and Isaac went to the mountaintop, God had a surprise!

God showed Abraham a ram whose horns were trapped in thorns.

God provided the ram for an offering.

Jesus' head was wrapped in a crown of thorns
   when God sacrificed His Son on the cross in our place.

God's people cried out to God when they were in Egypt.
God sent Moses and said, "Tell Pharaoh, 'Let My people go!'"
When Pharaoh said, "No!" God sent powerful plagues.
Pharaoh said "No!" nine times.
The last plague would kill the firstborn son in each family.
If a family painted a lamb's blood on the doorframe of their
    house, the firstborn sons in that house would be saved.
When the angel saw the blood, it passed over the house.
When Jesus died on the cross, His blood set us free from death.

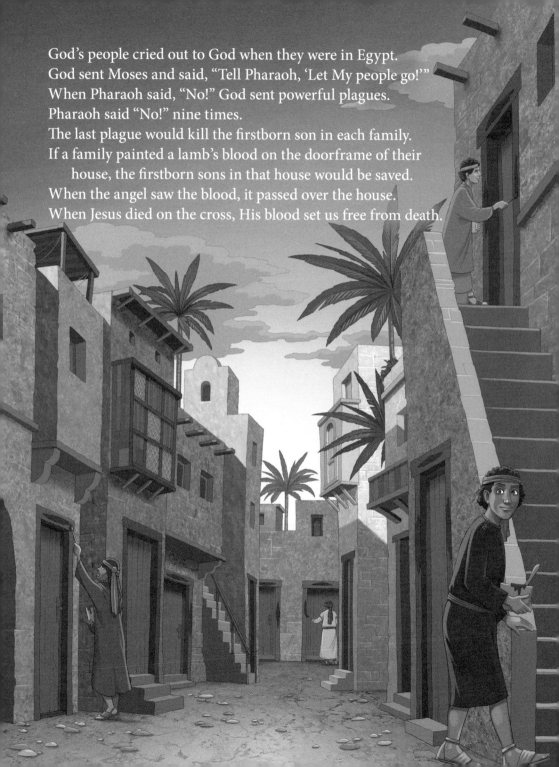

Goliath the giant challenged an Israelite, one of God's people, to fight him,
   but King Saul and all his soldiers were too scared to go.
Then young David heard the giant, and God made him very brave.
David knew that God would help him win the victory.
He grabbed a stone and ran toward Goliath, spinning his sling faster
   and faster.
The stone flew out of David's sling and struck the giant's forehead.
Goliath fell to the ground, dying at David's feet.
On the cross, Jesus, the Son of David, struck Satan's head.
Satan fell at Jesus' feet, soon to be chained in hell.

King Darius liked Daniel and trusted him to lead.
But the other leaders were jealous of Daniel.
They tricked the king into making a law that if someone prayed
    to anyone but the king, they would be thrown into the lions' den.
Daniel prayed to God. He was caught by the other leaders, who threw him
    into the lions' den and rolled a large stone in front of it to lock him in.
Early the next morning, the king rushed out and found Daniel alive
    and well.
After Jesus died on the cross, His body was laid in a tomb, and a large
    stone was rolled in front of the tomb.
Early on the first Easter Sunday, the women rushed to the tomb and found
    it empty: Jesus was alive and well.

In a little town called Bethlehem,
   God's Son, Jesus, was born.
Mary laid Him to sleep in a manger.
Angels told shepherds the good news.
The shepherds rushed to Bethlehem.
They saw baby Jesus, then returned and
   told everyone what they had heard and seen.

Jesus grew up in Nazareth.
He learned to be a carpenter at Joseph's side.
When He was thirty years old, Jesus left His shop
    and traveled to John the Baptist at the Jordan River.
John baptized Jesus, and the Holy Spirit came upon Jesus.
God the Father said, "This is My beloved Son,
    with whom I am well pleased."
Jesus' ministry of teaching and healing had begun.

Many sick people came to see Jesus:
    the blind who couldn't see,
    the deaf who couldn't hear,
    people who could not walk,
    and others with high fevers.
Jesus healed them all.
When He comes again on Judgment Day,
    He will make all who believe in Him alive, healthy, and strong.

Jesus teaches us all about God and His kingdom.
He shows us our sins and how He came to earth
    and died on the cross to save us from them.
He teaches us how to love God first
    and how to love one another the way God wants us to.
He teaches us that He will come again
    and make everything new and good forever.

Jesus went to the cross in our place.
He suffered to save us from our sins.
When He died, He destroyed Satan's work,
    bringing the giant to his knees.
He turned away God's anger
    so God forgives us and loves us
    as His own sons and daughters.

Early on the first Easter Sunday morning, Jesus rose from the dead.
When the women came to see Him, angels told them, "He is not here."
They looked where His body once lay,
    but there was nothing but empty strips of cloth.
Then, turning around, they saw Jesus Himself.
By His death and resurrection, Jesus set us free
    so we can live with Him forever.

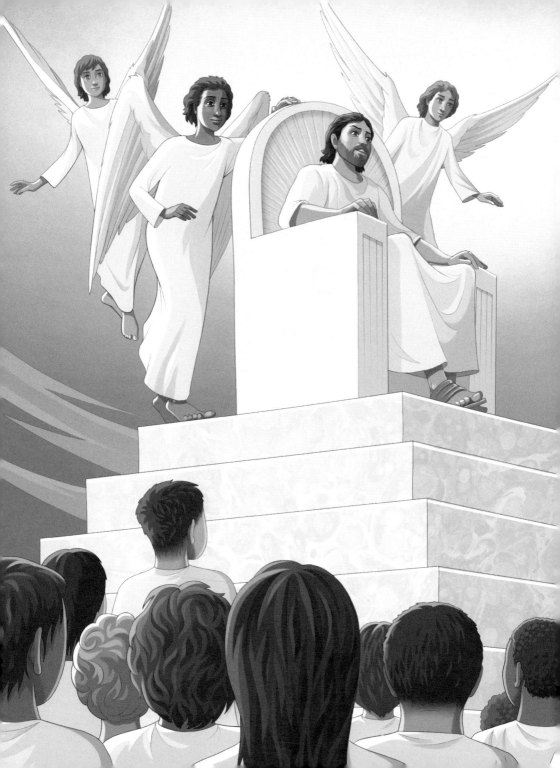

After Jesus rose from the dead,
    He appeared to His disciples.
Then, after forty days,
    He rose up and ascended into heaven.
One day, Jesus will come back
    with all His holy angels.
He will judge all people, gathering all who
    believe in Him to stay with Him forever.

We who believe in Jesus will shine in glory
and live together with Jesus forever.
We will see the angels and sing with them.
There will be a garden; the tree of life will always have fruit.
Jesus will make everything new,
and the world will be perfect again
like it was when it was brand new.
Come soon, Lord Jesus!